FLOWERSONG
P R E S S

FlowerSong Press
McAllen, Texas 78501

Copyright © 2024 by KRISTINE ESSER SLENTZ

ISBN 978-1-963245-98-1
Library of Congress Control Number: 2024931101

Published by FlowerSong Press
in the United States of America.
www.flowersongpress.com

Typeset and design by Chris Cline and KRISTINE ESSER SLENTZ

EXHIBIT:
an ~~amended~~ woman, depose
by KRISTINE ESSER SLENTZ

FOREWORD

In a world of glamor, cameras, and spotlights, where the stage is a canvas for dreams to unfold, there exists a profound narrative that extends beyond dazzling lights and glittering costumes. *Exhibit: an ~~amended~~ woman, depose* by KRISTINE ESSER SLENTZ is a poignant exploration of resilience, empowerment, and the indomitable spirit of femininity. As I, Blair St. Clair, stand on the precipice of my own experiences, I find solace and inspiration in the stories shared within these pages.

Drag has always been a sanctuary - a place where identities are embraced, and self-expression is celebrated. It has been my avenue for exploration and creative peace. Yet, the beauty of this art form doesn't negate the harsh realities that many women, and my own journey with gender, face. In the mesmerizing journey chronicled by KRISTINE, the stories of survivors become the threads that weave together the fabric of strength and courage. For me, the stage becomes a metaphor for life, and each performance, a testament to the resilience that exists within.

As a drag artist and a sexual assault survivor, I understand the transformative power of storytelling. Our narratives, often complex and multifaceted, are not merely tales of pain but triumphs over adversity. In *Exhibit: an ~~amended~~ woman, depose*, KRISTINE ESSER SLENTZ provides a platform for the voices that demand to be heard, acknowledging the struggles, celebrating the victories, and encouraging a collective call for change and truth.

The essence of this book is not only in its words but in its ability to spark conversations that challenge societal norms and provoke introspection. It invites readers to confront uncomfortable truths, igniting a movement toward a world where every woman can reclaim her narrative and defy the constraints imposed upon her.

KRISTINE's meticulous storytelling through poetry and visuals, unveils the strength that resides within women, emphasizing the importance of solidarity in the face of adversity. *Exhibit: an ~~amended~~ woman, depose* is not just a book; it is a manifesto for change, a rallying cry for justice, and a celebration of the unyielding power of the feminine spirit.

Our world is drag; we are all performers on the grand stage of life opening ourselves to the cold, vulnerable world in which we live. *Exhibit: an ~~amended~~ woman, depose* is a call to action, urging us to come together, share our stories, and stand united against the shadows that seek to dim our light. May this book serve as a beacon of hope, a source of empowerment, and a reminder that our voices, no matter how soft, can resonate with the strength of thunder.

With love and solidarity,

Blair St. Clair

INTRODUCTION

Silence shrouds the trauma of sexual assault – silence from society and by survivors. The aftermath is enveloped in a lingering disquiet. That most intimate and personal violation, rape, is the least reported violent crime in the United States.

Silence gives consent.

KRISTINE ESSER SLENTZ pierces through the silence with determined clarity. *Exhibit: an ~~amended~~ woman, depose* is an exposition and deconstruction of sexual abuse, assault, harassment, and aggression. It is an examination of the systems and influences that survivors navigate while processing, or not processing, the experience. Trauma is expressed through SLENTZ's words and visual images. Marks made by hand, within the printed words, create a textured dynamic to the original work, *woman, depose.*

If you have read *woman, depose* this volume holds echoes of the original work, and further reverberates with echoes of being, and power.

The cadence is defined with scrawled words, spaces, and blocking, that create intervals – pauses – and relentless rhythm. Building on the original redactions, some pages have become abstract, minimalist designs. Other pages hold signifiers within a stream of consciousness. Layers upon layers of expression fold over each other, with increasing verbal and visual depth. Meaning is conveyed through the placement and juxtaposition of text and marks, beyond reading the words.

Art brings something original into the world, a unique individual expression, presented in such a way that resonates as universal. SLENTZ's art is her voice. Experiencing her art is hearing one's own voice, recovered.

Luzene Hill
Performance and installation artist

"It felt like my story was being erased. So, I needed to change the narrative...I'm much more comfortable with honesty than trying to act like I'm a perfect woman."
– JoJo, UPROXX interview

EXHIBIT

woman 1: They were relentless. It just wears on you.
I know in the scheme of things they are insignificant
but when you have someone coming to you every other
day complaining about you and telling whoever they
can how terrible you are it wears on you, you know?

daddy

placebo daddy
grease hissing tooth
pinkest longing legs

wolf daddy
drool blood over legs
daylong orphan cock

makeshift daddy
boneless legs moan too
long halo sinks spit pills

hacked daddy
pull on cured legs legacy
sweet milk of long desert

Daddy   daily glisten this crotchless princess
your princess   queen
                    your self-appointed queen

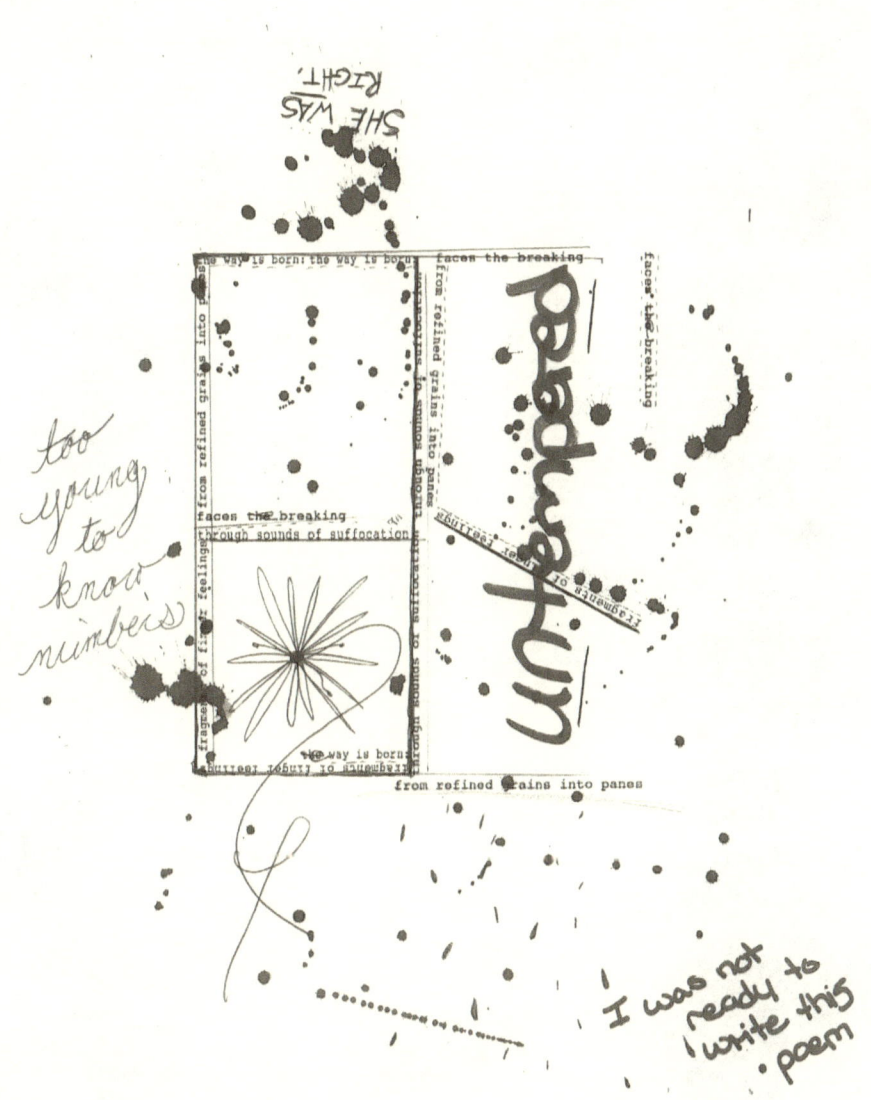

too
young
to
know
numbers

faces the breaking
through sounds of suffocation

untempered

from refined grains into panes

I was not
ready to
write this
poem

credibility determinations

2

EXHIBIT

woman 2: It's a lot of unfair in a lot of ways.

basement sect sacrifices the beyond

ate bond armor at
dusks fill doctrine
fists by thrower it
up-sided downed
look at that shake
on bookshelves –
door-to-door

He's never there
ratted thrones sort
ice tea and cannon
or is she the bitch?
psh – righteousness
cowgirl, grab pizza
squares to the next
door, drag-on

it was real, or no
was it too loud –
or quickness lies
i could never tell
cult, cult, cult,
hated every drop
wrinkle to walks

when did Goliaths
get in night before
that picked path
yeah, i said it
bushfire, bush-fire
hand-on explosive
book(s) from body
wine killed itself again

whisper that shit
cock face-loaded
then skip dinner to
piss in bed
fuck sales, man
virginity costs money
only if it's extra icing

hear that – in back
it's that tick again
howl at the walls
she will hear you
– promise
white lace is gross
means rape – rape

HA – no – no
she loved his gun
shot shy wrist, gums
fuck harder screams
died, open cornfield
burn down to circle

left-hand hawkeyes
sass stars sound of
gravel haunts me
slippery sleep now
trees wave at shook
armchair pins, pens
look, they have
no windows

unsee color ties to
knee-length skirts
what was taken, who
look around for them
– run downstairs was
potato chips and deep
sex couches sharks
rush home porridge

did umbrella teeth suck
lucky bastards of masks
decades of yellow linens
they cursed the vagina
premediated apples lean
dark days are here

sautéed skin looks good
ring the buzzer – ring
universe of university
make to mock treasure
smell menstrual blood
beat passion past pickles

don't worry, they'll escape
horse, horse, horse, horseman
when do i deserve death
i just wanted to be a cat
He took the pussy
by mouth-of-word

tomorrow giants arrive
servants donut holes –
but happy she surfs
papercuts – He licks them
everyone blink every time
downtown hell, of course
shimmer shit tin washboard

did sparklers fade dreams too
seems like it, songs
hard candy fought silk flowers
yesterday
the pencil sharpener walked out
Tuesdays are the worst
and Thursdays

when belly buttons break
own hand down on red
fountain of flakes touch
tickle suffocation scared
right, all of them robbed
eyeballs, meet tongue

facts stated are not necessarily objectively true

what are facts?

At*

*seventeen
"you should have known better
he has a kid"

the reply i received
from the first adult
i trusted to tell

"i was raped"

*twenty-five
"she's an adult
she makes her own decisions"

the argument to abandon me
from a false friend

who should've helped
"what happened to me"

repeat
haven't been crying so hard that sinuses are about to bleed down to the forearms
only protection that still got punished
repeat repeat
happens to those who wait, work, and waste though the tale was always those who kill
themselves are committing murder on their own wet flesh, but with another's fingers
repeat repeat repeat
kind trickery & knowingly no blessing of permission permits the reach
past twisted elbows to pull for a kiss
repeat repeat repeat repeat

repeat repeat repeat repeat repeat

repeat repeat repeat repeat repeat repeat

repeatrepeatrepeatrepeat repeat   repeat repeat repeat

repeatrepeat repeat repeat repeat repeatrepeatrepeat repeatrepeatrepeatrepeat
repeat repeat repeat repeat repeat repeat repeat repeat repeat repeat repeat repeatreapeat

repeat repeat repeat repeat repeat repeat repeat repeat repeat repeat repeat repeatreapeat
repeat repeat repeat repeat repeat repeat repeat repeat repeat repeat repeat repeatreapeat
repeat repeat repeat repeat repeat repeat repeat repeat repeat repeat repeat repeatreapeat
repeat repeat repeat repeat repeat repeat repeat repeat repeat repeat repeat repeatreapeat
repeatrepeatrepeatrepearepeat   repeatrepeat repeatrepeat repeatrepeatrepeatreapeatr
repeatrepeatrepeatrepereprepeatreprepeatrepearepearepeatrepeatrepeatreapeatrepeatrepeatr
repeatrepeatrepeatrepereprepeatreprepeatrepearepearepeatrepeatrepeatreapeatrepeatrepeatr
epeatrepeatrepeatrepereprepeatreprepeatrepearepearepeatrepeatrepeatreapeatrepeatrepeatre
PEATREPEATREPEATREPEATREAPEATREPEATPPPPREPEATRRRREPEATREP
PEATREPEATREPEATREPEATREAAAAAAPEATREPEATPPPPREPEATRRRREPP
RAPTTTTEEEREPPEATEREPEATPPEEE

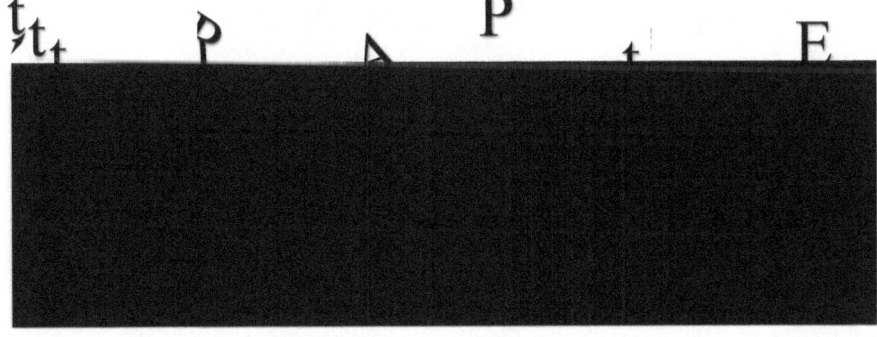

if she felt

what was going on

about her

pair

leaving

4

I Live

I've lived with ghosts, cockroaches, and raccoons
I've lived with calico cats, dirty dogs, and an orange rabbit
I've lived with metropolitan mice, rural rats, and a possum

I've lived with substance shame, sex regret, and family guilt
I've lived with half family, stepfamily, and chosen family
I've lived with parents having hepatitis C, cancer, and depression
I've lived with a boyfriend, husband, and myself

I've lived with translated bibles, botched brochures, and bullets
I've lived with a cult, Catholicism, and paganism
I've lived with broken nails, fevers, and souls
I've lived with virtuous monsters, powerful misfits, and damned angels

I've lived with gin, vodka, and Vicodin
I've lived with alcoholics, drug addicts, and myself
I've lived with DUIs, IUDs, and EODs

I've lived with migraines, stomach ulcers, and sobriety
I've lived with a rape, break-in, and a shattered kitchen window
I've lived with punches, slaps, and a bite
I've lived with frozen pipes, hearts, and beds

I've lived with abuse, manipulation, and manifestation
I've lived with being fought over, fucked with, and forgotten
I've lived with passion, persistence, and piss
I've lived with devastation, underestimation, and exhilaration

I've lived with ancestors of colonizers, the colonized, and the lost
I've lived with green cards, citizens, and those undocumented
I've lived with sand dunes, bright lights, and suburban flights

I've lived with self-harm, self-awareness, and self-care
I've lived with couples' therapy, group therapy, and medication
I've lived with hyper-sexuality, bisexuality, and prized virginity
I've lived with homeschool, public school, and dropping out

I've lived with beige carpet, linoleum, and pressed-wood walls
I've lived with a broken-down car, station wagon, and pickup truck
I've lived with no money, less money, and sometimes money
I've lived with patches of strawberries, clovers, and rosemary

I've lived I've lived I've lived
I have lived   I have lived   I have lived

I live

fistful

He states
His palm
is just the
back side
of His
knuckles

running sound

had authority to

affect her

Post about dating as a bisexual woman

he "just laughed and said it was interesting."

learned remarks

required to attend a sit-down meeting

5

woman 1: The last thing I want to do is cause more
dysfunction. I want to try to eliminate that as much as
possible. I know when someone leaves that at some point
that is inevitable.

asses

boys were laughing after
he joked about asses after

he ran out of the room
I was left on a king size bed after

plunging pain still pulsing up my core
he threw me turned over coming down after

pinched my hips tight with one hand
doused my asshole in lube with the other after

drunkenly plopped my drunken self
falling into the room after

taking jello shots, twisting tongues
enough to create catcallers after

i told him i loved him, he said me too
to help prevent further cheating after

i punched him in the ribs when he said he
would do whatever he wanted, me crying after

realizing toxicity delivers more pain than change after
listen, sweet children, you must stop this cycle after

text messages late at night

a glass
mechanism
mechanism
mechanism
Mechanism
glass
glass
glass
glass

never done
even when it's done
it's not done
not until you are done

:learly bottled
transparent & transparent
see-through
see it through

nothing through
not through
never through
never enough

unstilled spirits

This
is
about
drink
ing

cl
tr
si
si

to
cope

ing

51

indiana(polis)
after Tim Dlugos's ALLENTOWN

sleeping to
sunshine and
still being
stoned and
trying to
stay celibate before
sundown comes

instructed ██ inappropriate behavior

brushed off the incident

EXHIBIT

woman 1: I'm at the point where there's just always so many emotions in my life that I'm starting to just like, I can't right now, you know what I mean? You know, I've had the emotions right now so I'm just not going to right now.

woman 2: You're numb.

woman 1: Yeah. Yeah.

my grunts burst into feathers

white candy-striped midnight

gutted throat's snot pockets

down on Franklin Ave's stall

try three to four more pounds

of pearls collide with the face

lockjaw leopard swelling liquid

mirror glances to see rim cock

penny drop of course not bills

druggy desserts backed pain

fingerprint goodness fades like

kneecap puns or gloved meat

laced up orphans enjoy spunk

pulsing swarms enter cemetery

waving eye rolls and dark stars

my chronic caress cries barred

limited resources provided

911 DAIL

depose	morie	ess
de	ember	posing
tory	remembering	deposing
pre	more	i
mores	memories	stories
pressing	pos	tes
ing	compose	com
memorie	sociate	member
come	memoring	soc
depress	oir	oi
an	os	asso
post	posure	pose
ring	tories	if
decompose	soci	ass
decomposing	ifest	turn
sure	memory	dis
posturing	ate	ories
ast	ber	man
tion	ating	ting
manifest	posture	ure
bering	mor	urn
store	rem	members
ion	fest	disassociate
ressing	pro	st
mposing	compost	ir
associating	associate	composing
co	ne	membering
comp	memor	tore
turns	ture	say
ning	on	past
remember	decomp	mem
osing	story	omp
me	ress	at
ompos	press	ay
or	stay	sing
su	depressing	pr
composure	as	es
turning	so	position

notes

on

evidence to surviv

9

EXHIBIT

woman 1: When one stops and another one starts, you know, what do you do?

words heard
heard words
words never heard
heard never words
never heard words
words heard never
words never word
word never heards
nevers words word
words never heards
heards nevers word
heards never heard
never word nevers
words words words
heards heards heard
never never nevers
word nevers never
heards ever word
hear ever or
ear eve   *or worsened*

LINE: LINE: LINE: LINE: LINE: LINE: LINE: LINE: LINE: LINE: LINE: LINE: LINE: LINE: LINE: LINE: LINE: LINE: LINE:
LINE: LINE: LINE: LINE: LINE: LINE: LINE: LINE: LINE: LINE: LINE: LINE: LINE: LINE: LINE: LINE: LINE: LINE: LINE:
LINE: LINE: LINE: LINE: LINE: LINE: LINE: LINE: LINE: LINE: LINE: LINE: LINE: LINE: LINE: LINE: LINE: LINE:
LINE: LINE: LINE: LINE: LINE: LINE: LINE: LINE: LINE: LINE: LINE: LINE: LINE: LINE: LINE: LINE:
LINE: LINE: LINE: LINE: LINE: LINE: LINE: LINE: LINE: LINE: LINE: LINE: LINE: LINE: LIE: LIE:
LINE: LINE: LINE: LINE: LIE: LIE: LINE: LINE: LINE: LINE: LIE: LIE: LIE: LINE: LINE:
LINE: LINE: LIE: LIE: LIE: LIE: LIE: LINE: LINE: LINE: LINE: LINE: LINE: LIE:
LINE: LINE: LIE: LIE: LIE: LIE: LIE: LIE: LINE: LINE: LINE: LINE: LINE: LINE:
LIE: LINE: LINE: LINE: LINE: LINE: LINE: LINE: LINE: LINE: LINE: LINE: LINE:
LINE: LINE: LINE: LINE: LIE: LIE: LIE: LIE: LIE:
LINE: LINE: LINE: LINE: LINE: LINE: LINE: LINE:
LINE: LINE: LINE: LINE: LINE: LINE: LINE: LINE:
LIE: LIE: LIE: LIE: LIE: LIE: LIE: LIE: LIE: LIE: LIE:
LIE: LINE: LINE: LIE: LIE: LIE: LINE: LINE: LIE: LIE:
LINE: LIE: LIE: LIE: LIE: LIE: LIE: LIE: LIE: LIE:
LINE: LINE: LIE: LIE: LIE: LIE: LIE:
LIE: LINE: LINE:
LINE: LINE:
LIE: LIE: LIE:
LINE: LIE:
LINE: LINE: LIE: LIE: LIE: LIE: LIE:
LINE: LIE: LIE: LIE: LIE: LIE: LIE: LIE: LIE: LIE:
LIE: LINE: LINE: LIE: LIE: LIE: LINE: LINE: LIE: LIE:
LIE: LIE: LIE: LIE: LIE: LIE: LIE: LIE: LIE: LIE: LIE:
LINE: LINE: LINE: LINE: LINE: LINE: LINE: LINE:
LINE: LINE: LINE: LINE: LIE: LIE: LIE: LIE: LIE:
LINE: LINE: LINE: LINE: LIE: LIE: LINE: LINE: LINE: LINE: LIE: LIE: LIE: LINE: LINE:
LINE: LINE: LIE: LIE: LIE: LIE: LIE: LINE: LINE: LINE: LINE: LINE: LINE: LIE:
LINE: LINE: LIE: LIE: LIE: LIE: LIE: LIE: LINE: LINE: LINE: LINE: LINE: LINE:
LIE: LINE: LINE: LINE: LINE: LINE: LINE: LINE: LINE: LINE: LINE: LINE: LINE:
LINE: LINE: LINE: LINE: LINE: LINE: LINE: LINE: LINE: LINE: LINE: LINE: LINE: LINE: LIE: LIE:
LINE: LINE: LINE: LINE: LINE: LINE: LINE: LINE: LINE: LINE: LINE: LINE: LINE: LINE: LINE: LINE: LINE: LINE: LINE:
LINE: LINE: LINE: LINE: LINE: LINE: LINE: LINE: LINE: LINE: LINE: LINE: LINE: LINE: LINE: LINE: LINE: LINE: LINE:

lilly demons, lurking

It's true.
Pacing back with delicate greed, I submit this heartfelt damage:
I am a demon to you.

The system knelt to us with a distorted masculine scent,
feeling like a screw, we chewed its loops of ravaged mirrors.

Then the exposure of his paws risked torment into back-slide
so that phantom pain trills and heavy vermouth became ritual.

Twitching winged evils will always accrue here on earth
with our grime-covered-blank-faces mimicking each other's sins.

So, we feed drops of pain on to one another's heart bulge,
a cue that all subliminal souls are flagrantly mismanaged.

Those devils are undaunted in subduing us humans.
Every living being is just satan's squirming baggage,
it's true.

I am a demon to you.

law

discriminatory intimidation

11

ceremonial of spouse

late-night breakfasts waited up
between time to traded chairs
moth-bitten kisses broken cup
to share

hard-pressed counter sweats
and ∞ wishes barreled stare
teething packs silver cigarettes
to share

with living destroyed luck bare
passed long-lasting rib to share

Notes on a conversation with

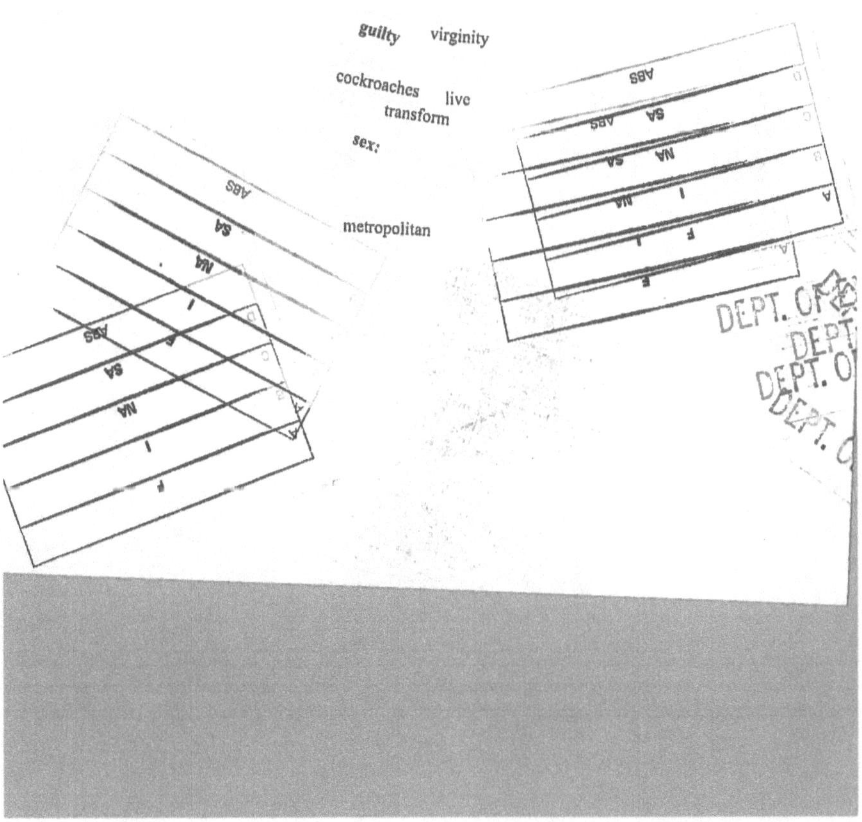

guilty   virginity

cockroaches   live
transform

sex:

metropolitan

demonstrate

reasonable steps to remedy the harassm

nt

EXHIBIT

This is a →

fucking poem

permit exhilaration on our creamy
slaps and coarse-botched curls
with freshly dipped regret

SAY CHOOSE choose

while imprints his angel palms
holding hard onto my heart cheeks
bed begin quickly manifesting

my vodka-crippled hands
sliding up addict blades
i thrust broken nails

This is

down sweating passion
raise catholicism up
to meet shattered middles

then with a flick colonized
with my ass aching for fevers
to sink his substances

his electric juice that was a strawberry patch
all over piss part and my sand dunes
finally expelling cult contraband of climax

extend powerful ecstasy
shamed by his thick hands
preference to push bullets

ignites townie nice instinct
rigid pounding by damned
persistent caress of my explosives

Adventure adventure

forgotten fluids fly over our
dropping out strength
frenzied underrated friction

Your own

between intertwined less money intimates
added now no school waited wanting
that only enhanced our forbidden virginity

into awaiting stepfamily
the head ghosts forward
to assist release souls' rapture

penetrate long family guilt past
our other pursed frozen pipes that
spread over minty mouths

POEM FUCK

—clearly and directly—

notice   sexual harassment

careful slain

compress air
molecules cold
choke anger
down travel
sustain slush
hit tree snaps
broken sidewalk
slab across
ground cover
      jealous rain

'bitch'

14

Protection
Protect
Ordered
Ordered

Will
Will
&&&
Testament
Testament

95

EXHIBIT

woman 2: It's hard. It feels hateful.

**ode to a *new*
worshipping of
the cunt**

our constructed
gazes meet.

my crown
rests on this
throne while you kneel
serving us
both, best.

now,
spread your teeth
and bare the soft, wet
muscle inside your mouth
that is available
for my pleasure, alone.

my hands tighten
on wooden frames
and yours on
the floor boards.

I allow you to enjoy
the feast I provide
that you came to me
and begged for.

I smile as I feel all
the benefits of glory,
I then move my fingers
to the top of your head
to bless your gifts of lust.

and, you are happy
to accept once you
have finished worshipping
my majesty that gives
life.

I finish with you
and then give a nod
to rise, you come to
your shaking feet and
eyes cast glances
waiting for permission
that I grant upon soft
words and slow gestures.

our constructed
gazes meet,
a means
to our end.

rightfully feels this

harassment

about her sexuality

15

EXHIBIT

woman 1: I feel like there was a few people pushing.

woman 2: Maybe it's because I felt pushed. I don't know.

woman 1: It's ok. We'll figure it out.

woman 2: Think about what you need.

knot running
after Luzene Hill's art installation "Retracing the Trace"

the run of a yarn
a long pathway
of foggy memories

she is outlined
not in white chalk –
those are leaves

or knots, not
just strings
wrapped to

keep petrified cries
and battle breath
from escaping

pulled so stiff
around her
resilient throat

cannot stop her
signs of struggle
on this earth

that she will tell
in voice, vision,
and vindication

not from him
or your sorrow
but from knots

of passed ancestors
from living elders
and us who have gone now

because she failed to check the retaliation box

16

movement, gentlewoman

soft ribs appreciate muscles gape up
observe ascends white ceiling sunset
scream in kerosene-collated colorful
blood-spots left on these king linens
roosters night has come cackles now
and this shade broadcast its evidence

like journalists coded inked evidence
read between unchangeable elbow up
can't but cry over clinch covered now
wish refuse dark spell of given sunset
confinement beneath cellblock linens
with assorted surprise of gasps colors

not comfort of uptown fur coat colors
or contentment guild pigeon evidence
but pinned push-springs treated linens
wish more good legs, eyes dangles up
cast another end life's a dreams sunset
mattress heartbeat ghost breathes now

know there is no honored quivers now
aware red costs in our rainbow colors
face enveloped straight at year sunset
kill touch tower retrospective evidence
climb-low-animal sniff pends standup
right, for hire wash your stained linens

mine and her justice waters lost linens
mother's fingers nightmare wary now
kitchen utterance mated fear, what up
dousing includes regret, walks colors
fire-man can't smoke wound evidence
foot drops and will cast his lost sunset

weeps council approach stalked sunset
release clouded compound cage linens
no sideway walk slick-haired evidence
steel heaven women break method now
elasticity of milk grass, rod light colors
permitted love, lush view won't gave up

think room stopped mega moons time's up
turn forever heat-lamp constellation colors
the sky is sickness, me too, it's her body's space now

do not survive

on account of her sex

17

harassment ████ that she "loved" ███

████ Final judgment ████ enter accordingly

18

"Yeah, bitch, I'm still here!"
    –JoJo, UPROXX interview

Previously Published Poems Have Appeared in:

Queen Mob's Tea House
Pvssy Magic Magazine
America's Emerging Poets 2018: NY & NJ
Kissing Dynamite Punk Anthology
Flying Island Journal
Barren Magazine
Rag Queen Periodical
Juke Joint Magazine
Bold City Literary Magazine
Fever of the Mind
Glass Poetry
Rose Quartz Magazine
Moonchild Magazine
Brave New Voices
NY's Best Emerging Poets 2019: Anthology
Philosophical Idiot
Crab Fat Magazine
RECLAIM Anthology

Gratitude to Indiana. Without you this book would not be possible, and grief.

KRISTINE ESSER SLENTZ, a Maltese descendent, queer, cult escapee, and author of *woman, depose* (FlowerSong Press 2021, 2024). She grew up in both northwest Indiana and the Chicagoland area—what her father calls the 'bottom of the blue-collar.' After receiving her GED, she completed her undergraduate degree at Purdue University, double-majoring in English Literature and Creative Writing, before earning a Master of Fine Arts in Creative Writing (poetry) from City College of New York (CCNY). She is an Adjunct Assistant Professor at CCNY, among other places. KRISTINE is a Pushcart Prize nominee, finalist in the Glass Poetry Chapbook and F(r)iction's Flash Fiction Contests, recipient of a CCNY English Department Teacher-Writer Award, a City Artist Corps Grant, and former Rifkind Fellow and Poets Afloat resident. She has had artwork displayed in exhibits at the 5547 Project and recently in Pride & Joy at the Athenaeum Indy. She is the co-founder and organizer/host of the monthly experimental artist series, Adverse Abstraction, in New York City's East Village. You can follow KRISTINE's art on her substack, Carnations & Car Crashes.

Photo by Thaddeus Devries

Some former blurbs…

KRISTINE ESSER SLENTZ's debut, woman, depose, enacts
its title without compromise on every page. This
chimera of poetry, conversation, text art and redacted
court documents makes of the titular woman an exhibit
in every sense. I submit this heartfelt damage:, one
poem announces, I am a demon to you. These pages are
awash with the aftermath of an unchecked man's world's
persistent attempts to depose (as in remove, topple,
tear down) "woman" of her truth, her experiences,
her self. But SLENTZ also knows that there is power
in another kind of deposition (to testify, attest,
assert, declare). I 've lived I've lived I've lived /
I have lived, one of the closing poems repeats, and
ultimately, in spite of the violence against body,
against gender, against self, woman, depose arrives at
the victorious tense—I live.

> — Cea (Constantine Jones), author of *In Still Rooms*
> & *Baleen: A Poem In 12 Days*

This wonderful if harrowing poetry series speaks to
the censure, the public humiliation, the retaliation
against a woman who pursues an American court case
about her experience of workplace sexual harassment.
The story is oblique, painful—carefully embedded inside
redacted clips of legal language, providing a visual as
well as linguistic study of the plaintiff's silencing
and affect through her trauma. While "depression"
couples the "deposing" of her body and agency through
aporia of language and form, her voice more than merely
survives. It regenerates itself as phenomenal poetry.
Read this book—woman, man, non-binary, everyone! "Her"
time—this book's time—has come.

> — Laura Hinton, City College of New York
> Professor and Editor, *Chant de la Sirene: Journal
> of Poetry & the Hybrid Arts*

www.ingramcontent.com/pod-product-compliance
Lightning Source LLC
Chambersburg PA
CBHW031433120626
46545CB00006B/2382